FREAKY FAMILIES

Chosen by David Orme

Illustrated by Peter Allen

MACMILLAN CHILDREN'S BOOKS

First published 2001
by Macmillan Children's Books
a division of Pan Macmillan Limited
20 New Wharf Road, London N1 9RR
Basingstoke and Oxford
www.panmacmillan.com

Associated companies throughout the world

ISBN 0 330 39207 7

A CIP catalogue record for this book is available from the British Library.

Printed by Mackays of Chatham plc, Chatham, Kent.

Contents

You Little Monster!
Ian Larmont   1

Grandma's Leather Handbag
John Coldwell   2

The Number Fifty-Seven
Matt Simpson   4

Fall Out
David Whitehead   6

A Tall Story
Marian Swinger   8

Hairy Story
Judith Nicholls   10

When Grandad Took Me to the Zoo
Brian Moses   12

Strange Relations
Peter Dixon   14

Watch Out, Our Granny's About!
David Harmer   16

The Spoons Music Man
Wes Magee   17

The Thingamybob
Pam Gidney   18

My Dad's a Dinner Lady
Celia Warren   20

Barmy Family
John Rice   21

Baby Talk
David Horner   22

Mi Grandad
Joan Poulson   24

My Nephew Paul
John Coldwell   26

Why are We Hiding in Here?
Trevor Millum   28

Another Tall Story
Clare Bevan   30

My Twin
John Cotton   32

My Dad
Roger Stevens   33

Aunties Galore
Michaela Morgan   34

Sullen Jane
Gareth Owen   36

Uncle Trunk
Gina Douthwaite   38

Grandma
Jan Dean   40

Mum For A Day
Paul Cookson   42

My Dad
Clive Webster   44

Baby Bert
Rex Andrews   46

Great-Aunt Polly
Moira Andrew   48

Man at the Door
Gus Grenfell   49

Jeffrey's Little Sister
Robin Mellor   50

A Freaky Family
Alan Priestley   52

A Friend for Tea
Gina Douthwaite   54

Run, Run!
Dave Ward   56

You Little Monster!

"You never put your clothes away,
You go out when it rains,
You bring home rubbish every day.
You fish for things in drains.

You are a little monster!"
His mother loudly roared,
But he **was** a little monster,
And he **knew** he was adored!

Ian Larmont

Grandma's Leather Handbag

Grandma's leather handbag is a very big
  container
Dad says it holds the kitchen sink with
  a double drainer.
The bag's so big that when she holds it
  on her lap
All you see of Grandma is the feather in
  her cap.

But if you need a hammer, some glue, a
  curtain ring,
She'll yell, "Hold on a minute, I've got the
  very thing."
I've seen her pull out bicycles, rice and
  rubber bands;
A thing for starting tractors and maps of
  foreign lands.

The last time that I visited, Grandma
    wasn't there,
But she'd left her leather handbag on her
    easy chair.
As no one was around, I thought I'd take
    peep.
I opened the bag and there was Grandma
    – fast asleep.

John Coldwell

The Number Fifty-Seven

What a to-do!
Oh, what a fuss!
My Auntie Pamela
Thinks she's a bus.

Look out the window!
The main road there!
Brum-brumming,
Brakes screeching,
Do you recognise her?

If you're uncertain,
If you're in doubt,
Just wait at the bus stop
And then you'll find out.

She's the big blue one
Wearing a bonnet
With a number Fifty-Seven
Painted upon it.

And if you want to go to town
To walk about the shops,
Just wave your left arm up and down
Until my Auntie stops.

Matt Simpson

Fall Out

Our dad built us a tree house.
It was really like no other.
We played there many happy hours – till

I
 f
  e
   l
    l
     o
      u
       t
        w
         i
          t
           h
            m
             y
              b
               r
                o
                 t
                  h
                   e
                    r

David Whitehead

A Tall Story

She's the strongest baby in all the land.
She can lift a horse with one big hand.
She can lift a car up with the other.
She's stronger than our dad and brother,
stronger than the strongest man,
but she isn't quite as strong as Gran
who can lift a house with one big hand,
the strongest gran in all the land.
She can lift an elephant with the other
but she isn't quite as strong as Mother
who can lift a ship with one big hand,
the strongest mother in all the land.
She can lift a whale up with the other.
And me, I'm not as strong as Mother,
but I'm the biggest fibber in all the
land . . .

Marian Swinger

Hairy Story

My Dad forgot to shave one day
and a few small hairs appeared.
He stroked his chin then said with a
   grin,
"I think I'll grow a beard!"

"Give us a hug!" cried Dad next day,
but we all disappeared.
Now Dad's chin's like scratchy pins
since he started to grow that beard!

"It's coming along," said Dad next week.
He'd really persevered,
so we all had to hug the hairy rug
that was Dad with his new beard!

"It's doing rather well!" said Dad.
He was looking really weird.
We watched him wash and comb and brush
and curl and twirl that beard.

"Now what do you think of it?" asked Dad,
and we all stood round and cheered;
for a small redbreast had made his nest
in the forest that was Dad's beard!

Judith Nicholls

When Grandad Took Me to the Zoo

When Grandad took me to the zoo,
Grandma said:
"You make sure he behaves himself . . ."
But he didn't.

He made faces at the monkeys,
he poked a penguin with his stick.
He went far too close to the tigers
and he woke up an angry snake.

He called the hippos names,
he dropped ice cream down his shirt.
He queued to go on the slide
till a zookeeper sent him out.

Then as he left he said,
"We'll come back as soon as we can."

"Sorry, Grandad," I answered,
"Next time I'm coming with Gran!"

Brian Moses

Strange Relations

I have not got relations
   (well only one or two),
so I've invented new ones
   like Tom and Auntie Pru.
My cousin Jack's a pop star,
Pru's a gipsy queen.
Uncle Joe's a pirate
and so is Auntie Jean.

   My Uncle Jim's a boxer
   My sister flies a plane
   Uncle Rob's a robber
   and ran away to Spain.

I love these new relations
   Josie
   Jane
   and Mo,
but best of all is Auntie
– my silly Auntie Flo!
Auntie Flo is crazy,
as crazy as a flea.

She dances in the roadway
   each day at half past three.
She lives on worms and water
   slugs and orange peel,
and that's my awful problem
'cos Auntie Flo is real!

Peter Dixon

Watch Out, Our Granny's About!

When Granny took up kick-boxing
We said, "Well that won't last."
But we've never seen her move
So lightly or so fast.
She whirls and twirls, leaps about
Throws snap kicks in the air.
You want to tell her she's too old?
You can try it – if you dare.

David Harmer

The Spoons Music Man

My uncle
made music with spoons.

He could play
any number of tunes.

He banged them
on knees and his nose.

He banged them
on elbows and toes.

My uncle
made wonderful tunes.

He made
magical music with spoons.

Wes Magee

The Thingamybob

My Uncle Fred's forgetful:
He's always losing things,
And when he does, he says to me,
"Where's my thingamy, Bob?"
But my name's Gavin.

I asked my Mum:
"Why does Uncle Fred
Always call me Bob?
My name's Gavin."

"I've never heard him call you Bob,"
Said Mum. "Are you quite sure?
He knows as well as I do
Your name's Gavin."

Just then Uncle Fred
Came in from the shed.
He looked suspiciously at me, and said,
"Well, what have you done
With my thingamy, Bob?"

"See?" I said, but
Mum only fell about laughing.
I wish I knew why.
She knows my name's Gavin.

So who's Bob?

Pam Gidney

My Dad's a Dinner Lady

My dad's a dinner lady
from twelve to one each day,
or a Lunchtime Supervisor,
as my teacher says to say,
but Dad *is* a dinner lady,
whatever she may say!

Celia Warren

Barmy Family

My mother is a slug burglar, she burgles
   slugs,
my father is a jug smuggler, he smuggles
   jugs,
my brother is a bug juggler, he juggles
   bugs,
my sister is a hug struggler, she struggles
   in hugs.

My uncle is a rug mugger, he mugs
   rugs,
my auntie is a plug tugger, she tugs
   plugs,
my cousin is a lug gurgler, she gurgles
   lugs,
my granny is a trug wuggler, she . . .

John Rice

Baby Talk

My baby brother says, "Gugga wugga
   wugga."
   Mummy says, "Oodle oodle oo."
My baby brother says, "Namma namma
   namma."
   Granny sings, "Coochie coochie
      coo."

My baby brother says, "Imma imma
   imma."
   The man next door goes, "Tickle
      ickle ickle."
My baby brother says, "Mumma umma
   umma."
   Auntie Jean says, "Oosa yickle
      pickle?"

My baby brother says, "Wubba wubba
   wubba."
   My big sister says, "Diffa daffa
      doo."
My baby brother says, "Dadda adda
   adda."
   Grandad, he goes, "Woo woo
      wooOOOO!"

My baby brother says, "Pshah pshah
   pshah."
   Daddy goes, "Nuggy nuggy noo."
My baby brother says, "Flaf flaf flah."
   I say, "Love you too!"

David Horner

Mi Grandad

It's like
the first day of summer
when mi grandad
comes to visit,

swinging down the street
with his duffel-bag
and in it all the things
he's brought home
to show us from his trip,
like the leaf he picked
from the topmost-tip
of a coconut palm.
Don't know yet
how he did it.

Sometimes he brings a recipe,
like one for the mango baked in rum.
Sometimes a song . . .
and he strums along,
one-man band,
as he sings . . .
old guitar never far from his hand.

It's like
the first day of summer
when mi grandad
comes to visit,
summer with the hottest sun
brightest rainbow,
in it.

Joan Poulson

My Nephew Paul

One of my nephews, whose name is Paul,
said, "I want to be a spider when I leave
   school."
So he found a dark corner in which to sit
Took out two needles and began to knit.
"I'm making a web to trap juicy flies."
He didn't catch one which was no
   surprise.
The other thing that he couldn't do at all
Was walk like a spider straight up a wall.
Paul said, "I'm not going to be a spider
   any more.
I want to be an elephant, like Steve next
   door."

John Coldwell

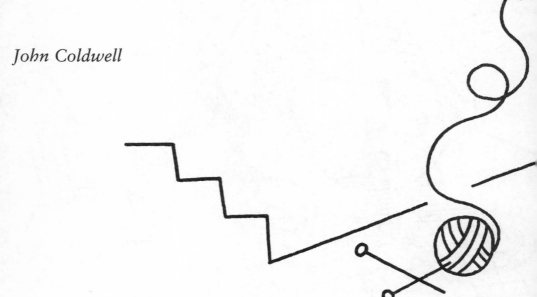

Why are We Hiding in Here?

Why are we hiding in here, Father?
Why are we hiding in here?
What monsters are coming, what men in
    black?
What grim clad figures on the attack?
Why are we hiding in here?

Why are we hiding in here?
Tell me the truth, Dad, please.
Is it the taxman?
Is it the axeman?
Is it the secret police?

Why are we hiding in here, Father?
Give me an answer, please.
Is it a giant slug?
Is it a doodlebug?
Is it that runny cheese?

SURPRISE!

WooF!
WooF!

There's nothing at all to fear, dear,
Nothing at all to fear.
It's just Aunt Gladys and Uncle Jim.
If we keep really quiet they won't know we're in.
That's why we're hiding in here, dear,
That's why we're hiding in here.

Trevor Millum

Another Tall Story

My uncle's a giant
Which sounds quite alarming.
It's true that he's huge
But his manners are charming.

He's built like a mountain
With thunderous feet,
But he fixes the rooftops
For friends in our street.

He's a fearsome protector
Of birds in their nests,
He rescues small creatures
From bullies and pests.

He's a two-legged taxi
As tall as a tree,
He carries old ladies
(Plus shopping) for free.

He's a sky-scraping playground,
A big, breathing slide –
We climb up his arms
For a white-knuckle ride.

He's an old-car-recycler
Who thumps with his thumb . . .
You think HE'S enormous?
You MUST meet my mum!

Clare Bevan

My Twin

My twin is a secret,
Seen briefly as a rule.
I'll glimpse her in a mirror,
Or glance at her in a pool.
A shiny spoon will catch her;
Then she's spread and round!
But in the deepest darkness
She's nowhere to be found.

When I see her,
Can she see me?

And when I can't see her,
Where can she be?

John Cotton

My Dad

My Dad's a cobbler.
He mends shoes.
He's my cobbling Dad.

He dropped the hammer on his toe.
He's my hobbling, cobbling Dad.

Dad had an argument with a customer.
He's my squabbling, hobbling, cobbling
   Dad.

So he made her a raspberry jelly.
He's my wobbling, squabbling, hobbling,
   cobbling Dad.

Then he ate it all himself.
He's my gobbling, wobbling, squabbling
   hobbling, cobbling Dad.

Roger Stevens

Aunties Galore

Have I got aunties? I've got stacks of 'em –
heaps and hordes and piles and packs of
   'em.
An abundance of aunties swarming
   round like ants
they make me jerseys, scarves, socks . . .
   and knitted underpants.
Everywhere I look there's an auntie
   sitting
an auntie telling stories,
nattering and knitting.
There are aunts in every cupboard,

aunties under the stairs,
aunties under the table,
aunts in all the chairs,
aunties watching telly,
aunties drinking tea,
aunties on the sofa . . .
and no room left for me.

Michaela Morgan

Sullen Jane

Oh what can be the matter
With sullen cousin Jane?
Is it something that she's eaten?
Is it something on her brain?

She frowns, she glowers, she grinds her
   teeth
Her jaw begins to jut
Her mouth turns down all tight and hard
Like a trap that's just snapped shut.

We do our best to cheer her up
But no matter how we try
Jane just wrinkles up her nose
And heaves a mournful sigh.

And if you try to comfort her
If you say a kindly word
She simply looks right through you
As if she hasn't heard.

Jane's got the sulky dumplings
She's gone all grumpified
She's dug herself a great big hole
And curled up tight inside.

At last my granny sighed and said,
"We can't go on like this
There's just one cure for sulky dumps
And I know what it is."

She made Jane tell her all her moans
And placed them in a tin
Then she put it in the backyard
Near the garden rubbish bin.

And now if Jane starts glowering
We fetch Granny's Grumble Tin
And put all Jane's sulks inside it
And replace them with a grin.

Gareth Owen

Uncle Trunk

His suits are sort of shabby,
grey, wrinkled, big and baggy,
his eyes and nose
all match his clothes,
his lips and ears are saggy.

His shape was never, ever meant
to suit a gent who's elegant
but we don't mind
if he's designed
to look more like an elephant.

Gina Douthwaite

Grandma

Grandma is teaching the trees to sing,
Building them giant harps
Stringing their branches with long
    humming wires
Painting their long limbs with pictures of
    larks.

Grandma is teaching the cows to dance,
Sewing them evening gowns,
Sprinkling sequins along their black tails,
Waltzing them over the downs.

Grandma is showing the frogs how to fly
So high on the circus trapeze.
She swoops to the music of wild violins
Then gracefully hangs by her knees.

Jan Dean

Mum For A Day

Mum's ill in bed today
so I said I'd do the housework
and look after things.
She told me it was really hard
but I said it would be dead easy.

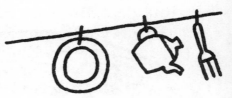

So . . .

I hoovered up the sink

Dusted the cat

Cooked my dad's shoes

Washed up the carpet in the dishwasher

Fed all the ornaments and pictures

Polished the steak and kidney pudding and chips

Ironed all the letters and parcels

Posted all the shirts and knickers

And last of all . . .
I hung the budgie out on the washing line to dry.

It took me all day
but I got everything finished
and I was really tired.

I'm glad Mum isn't ill every day
and do you know what?

So is the budgie.

Paul Cookson

My Dad

My dad.
He's good at football,
My dad.

My dad.
He's good at cricket,
My dad.

My dad.
He's good at snooker,
My dad.

My dad.
He's good at darts,
My dad.

My dad.
He's good at everything,
My dad.

My dad.
He's a big fibber,
My dad.

Clive Webster

Baby Bert

Baby Bert
plays in the dirt
he chucks it
he sucks it
he gets it in his shirt.

He chews old nails
he squashes snails
ties knots in wriggly worms.
He makes mud pies
with earth and flies.
He doesn't mind the germs.

With muddy hands
and filthy knees
his face is full of smiles;
But show him soap and water
and he'll run a thousand miles!

Rex Andrews

Great-Aunt Polly

Roly-poly, sugar-dusted
as a jam doughnut,
she wears round
wire-rimmed glasses
and her eyes shine
like wet pebbles.

She loves to gossip,
leans on the garden gate
toasting in the sunshine.
Her mouth is small,
painted red, pursed
as a ripe raspberry.

Great-Aunt Polly
puts on a squashy hat
and walks to church
on Sundays. She
knows everyone, hands
round mints to suck.

Moira Andrew

Man at the Door

Good morning. I'm your
great-great grandfather's oldest brother's
great nephew's mother's mother's
younger sister's youngest daughter's
third son's great grandfather's
second daughter's husband's
granddaughter's father's
son-in-law's grandson's
brother's mother's
husband's son's
grandfather's
daughter's
brother.

Hi, Dad!

Gus Grenfell

Jeffrey's Little Sister

My friend Jeffrey's little sister
thinks she's a dog.

She sits in the dog basket,
underneath the kitchen worktop,
and barks.

"What are you doing?"
I ask.
"Woof, woof."
she says.

She eats dog biscuits.
Not just the little round ones,
but the long ones shaped like a bone.

"It's on account of us
getting a dog at the same time
she was born,"
says Jeffrey's mum,
throwing her another dog biscuit.
"It's no problem, really."

The dog never says anything.
Just sits there,
his head on his paws,
and looks sad.

One day
Jeffrey's little sister
bit the postman on the leg.

"Right,"
said Jeffrey's dad.
"This has gone far enough.
You are not a dog.
Do you understand?
YOU ARE NOT A DOG!"

Jeffrey's little sister nodded,
climbed on to the kitchen worktop,
curled up and said,
"Meow!"

Robin Mellor

A Freaky Family

Father's nose is long and – beaky.
When Mum shouts her voice goes –
    squeaky.
Sister's dyed her hair all – streaky.
Brother's socks smell awful – reeky.

Auntie says that I'm too – cheeky.
Grandma's knees have gone all – creaky.
Grandad's looking quite – antiquey.

Beaky;
Squeaky;
Streaky;
Reeky.

Cheeky,
Creaky
and
Antiquey.

Does that make our family –

Freaky?

Alan Priestley

A Friend for Tea

Come in the kitchen. Meet my mum.
She's always jolly. Never glum.

Sings like the kettle on the stove,
gives hugs as warm as oven gloves.

Her chuckles make you want to die –
she wobbles like a custard pie,

and never cares if her hair flops
like one of those grey, stringy mops

into her swirling chocolate eyes.
They glisten with pretend surprise

ketchup →

each time I bring a friend for tea.
"*Yum, yum,*" she says. "*Is that for me?*"

then smiles, and licks her saucy lips –
you see, she loves my friends, *with chips*!

Gina Douthwaite

Run, Run!

Run, Run –
Here comes Mum,
She's got porridge in her hair.

Run, Run –
Here comes Mum,
She's found the spider on her chair.

Run, Run –
Here comes Mum,
And she knows who put it there!

Dave Ward